D1367098

MEL BAY PUBLICATIONS ● PACIFIC, MO. 63069

MEL BAY PUBLICATIONS ● PACIFIC, MO. 63069

MEL BAY PUBLICATIONS ● PACIFIC, MO. 63069

MEL BAY PUBLICATIONS ● PACIFIC, MO. 63069

MEL BAY PUBLICATIONS ● PACIFIC, MO. 63069

MEL BAY PUBLICATIONS ● PACIFIC, MO. 63069

Blank music manuscript paper with nine staves.

MEL BAY PUBLICATIONS ● PACIFIC, MO. 63069

MEL BAY PUBLICATIONS ● PACIFIC, MO. 63069

MEL BAY PUBLICATIONS ● PACIFIC, MO. 63069

MEL BAY PUBLICATIONS ● PACIFIC, MO. 63069

MEL BAY PUBLICATIONS ● PACIFIC. MO. 63069

MEL BAY PUBLICATIONS ● PACIFIC. MO. 63069

MEL BAY PUBLICATIONS ● PACIFIC, MO. 63069

MEL BAY PUBLICATIONS ● PACIFIC. MO. 63069

MEL BAY PUBLICATIONS ● PACIFIC, MO. 63069

MEL BAY PUBLICATIONS ● PACIFIC, MO. 63069